BABY HACKS HANDBOOK

HOW TO RAISE YOUR NEWBORN THE FUN AND EASY WAY

DRAGON FRUIT

MARIA LLORENS AND HUGO VILLABONA

Front Cover Image: ARaspopova/Shutterstock.com
Back Cover Image: Balandina Nadezshda/Shutterstock.com, kappacha/
Shutterstock.com, sidmay/Shutterstock.com
Cover Design: Elina Diaz
Interior Design, Theme and Layout: Elina Diaz, Roberto Nuñez and
Hugo Villabona

Excepting original infographics by Elina Diaz, and Roberto Nuñez all
icons and illustrations from www.shutterstock.com.

Maria Llorens and Hugo Villabona/Mango Media, Inc.
2525 Ponce de Leon, Suite 300
Coral Gables, FL 33134
www.mangomedia.us

Publisher's Note: This is a work of humor with a hint of self-help. The
authors wish to thank all the experts, guides, and experiences which
were considered during the writing process.

Baby Hacks Handbook / Maria Llorens and Hugo Villabona. -- 1st ed.
ISBN 978-1-63353-085-0

DISCLAIMER

Everybody keeps saying congratulations, but the truth is you're petrified. Very few things are as scary as the idea of being responsible for another human life. However, your fears end here. There is no need to worry anymore thanks to the Baby Hacks Handbook. This is the definitive guide for how to raise your newborn the fun and easy way. Combining time-tested family tips with modern applications on parenting, Baby Hacks packs a parental punch unlike anything out there. Whether you're a happily married couple, a single parent, or a first-time adopter, these hacks will make this new, scary, and above all, exciting chapter of your life a little bit easier.

Before we begin, and this cannot be stressed enough, make sure you stay up to date with your doctor visits. There is no hack for the expertise your doctor can offer you. This handbook is simply a collection of observations and ideas that will, hopefully, turn your transition into a new parent from a scary, overly advised mess into a fun and easy adventure. So next time a stranger on the street comes up to you to rub your belly (or your wife's belly – this book is for men, too) and offers up hours of joyful anecdotes, just pull out your copy of the Baby Hacks Handbook and they'll know you're in good hands.

"I am tomorrow, or some future day, what I establish today. I am today what I established yesterday or some previous day."

- James Joyce

CONTENTS

PREFACE

We live in a world where everything is constantly changing, evolving, and being posted online. In this age of mass communication, it becomes harder and harder to decipher between the helpful and the hampering (or the painful and the pampering). Long gone are the days when parenting advice only came from the in-laws. So what are anxious first-time parents to do? You could try searching online, because nothing screams ill-equipped like Googling "first-time mother" or "my girlfriend is pregnant," or my personal favorite "my wife's water broke…what do I do?" The truth is that rummaging through the endless vines of the internet like a wayward pirate can be exhausting and the last thing any new parent needs is to be more exhausted. So let the Baby Hacks Handbook do all the heavy lifting. But seriously, don't lift anything heavy if you're pregnant.

Adding to the confusion is the 21st century fact that the combination of scientific advancements, social acceptance, and monumental political decisions have resulted in a world where parenting is no longer a simple roadmap. Rewind the clock 50 years or so to a world where parenting was reserved for happily married suburban couples in Middle America. In vitro fertilization was 30 years away, gay marriage, let alone gay couples adopting, was the furthest thing from the White House's mind, and teen pregnancies were handled with shotgun weddings instead of MTV.

Today's parents range from hormone-driven teens to Viagra-steeped senior citizens and everyone you can imagine in between. The over saturation of sex is only partially responsible for new parents that brace for the unknown each year. And while birth rates are slightly down, there are still a reported 4 million babies born in the US each year. Just picture Oprah standing in a maternity lobby: "you get a baby, you get a baby, and you get a baby! Everybody gets a baby!"

So where do you turn as a rookie parent? The Baby Hacks Handbook. From the second you find out you're pregnant to every milestone you and your infant will experience, this book will help out.

Unsure what to name your offspring? Does that gooey marmalade spit that keeps bubbling so adorably on their chin stain carpets? How can you tell if they're hungry? All of these questions and more will be addressed so by the time you're done reading you'll be ready for whatever your new baby can throw at you…even if there are twins in there. So let's hack on!

CHAPTER 1 //
You're Pregnant

We Are Expecting

**You're Pregnant //
How to Tell Your Partner,
Friends, and Parents**

Whether you've been trying to get pregnant for a long time, or you just heard back from the adoption agency, or your doctor broke the news to you during a routine check-up, the fact is telling people you're having a baby can be thrilling and a little overwhelming. Some people might get offended if they're not the first one you call, while others will be quick to prod with a laundry list of questions you can't wrap you head around. Boy or a girl? What names are you considering? Will you breastfeed? How do you feel about spanking? Did you start a college fund yet? When will you get them an iPhone? Hopefully, these hacks will make this exciting and unprecedented time of your life a little simpler.

Have Fun!

Your partner, parents, or friends are the people that love you the most in the world. Regardless if this was a planned pregnancy or the result of a frisky night, the truth is that you'll need the support of these people more than ever. By making the news of your pregnancy a fun and creative reveal, you'll be establishing a healthy environment of support and comfort. Here are our top 5 quirky ways to tell the people you love that the family is growing.

Build the Crib:

There is no need to splurge on the luxury liner of cribs. A well-researched, safety-guaranteed crib can be found simply if you know where to look. Instead of hitting up the megastores, look at buying it at a warehouse. They have to follow the same regulations, but because there is no stocking fee the cribs are way more budget-friendly.

Text the Ultrasound:

If you can fight the urge and wait a little while, texting or posting a photograph allows you to get the message out to your closest friends and family at the same time.

Baby Coupon, Good for One Newborn:

For the DIY-inclined, making and printing a simple Baby Coupon can be a breeze. The expiration date can be set to the projected birth month while multiple copies can be mailed to friends and family.

Baby Gift Basket:

If your partner's birthday is coming up, or if the holidays are around the corner, you can purchase diapers, baby bottles, a couple of onesies, and a pacifier.

Dinner with a Baby Chair:

If you're looking for a simple and easy way to tell your partner or parents (or both), you can make dinner reservations and request that the table be set up with a highchair for a baby.

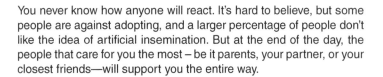

You never know how anyone will react. It's hard to believe, but some people are against adopting, and a larger percentage of people don't like the idea of artificial insemination. But at the end of the day, the people that care for you the most – be it parents, your partner, or your closest friends—will support you the entire way.

**You're Pregnant //
All Things Considered, Medically**

E verything about a new baby is expensive. Like vacationing in Copenhagen expensive. And there are a wide collection of hacks to help the budget-conscious parent…we'll get to those. However, there is one segment of the entire pregnancy paradigm where you should never cut corners: your doctor. These visits should be carefully calculated and consistent. But that doesn't mean we can't make them a little more 21st century-friendly.

Projected DOB:

Remember that faithful day in the 4th grade when your teacher finally entrusted you with the galactic power that was a palm-sized, solar-powered calculator? That day your life changed forever. Gone were the days of struggling with remainders, decibels and whatever an exponent is. That power you felt then has returned with the due date calculator. From apps to websites, you can find countless 21st century developments that tell you the date you'll be looking forward to. Some apps even provide personalized calendars that detail milestones your baby will be accomplishing while they rest for nine months.

Caregiver:

In the initial months of your pregnancy you'll be visiting your family physician, obstetrician and maybe a midwife. Like picking a new brand of detergent, you'll want the team of nurses and doctors to match your personality, your fears, and your hopes. After you've decided which direction you want to take your pregnancy, it's time to start scheduling your first prenatal appointment. FYI, most providers typically schedule the visit for when you're at least 8 weeks pregnant.

Baby Mortgage 101

Think of this section as a crash-course on financing the nine months leading up to the big day. The first thing you need to know is that maternity coverage is universal, to an extent, as a result of the Affordable Care Act. Basically, insurance plans must cover maternity care. Before this clause, which went into effect January 1, 2014, it was not unheard of to find expectant mothers without any coverage. Most of the time, this was a direct result of the expectant mother not having an employer-sponsored plan. Here is closer look at the numbers and how you can hack around them.

Out of Pocket:

Prior to January 1, 2014, the average out of pocket expenses for an uncomplicated pregnancy hovered around $10,000. A recent study detailed the total charges for maternal and new-born care to be right around $30,000.

Essential Benefit:

Maternity is part of the 10 essential benefits that health insurers must offer. So you can't be denied coverage, charged higher premiums, or discriminated against for being pregnant. Yet, keep in mind that states have a degree of discretion regarding what exactly has to and does not have to be covered.

Covered...not Free:

Regardless of your insurance plan, there is a 99% chance you'll be paying for a portion of this pregnancy. Welcome to parenthood. The baby isn't even born yet and they're already asking for a raise in their allowance. Become familiar with deductibles. High deductibles and premiums can be the difference between thousands of dollars during your pregnancy.

A good rule of thumb to keep in mind is that high deductible plans tend to offer reduced premiums which are great in the short run, but most likely they will result in a higher total out of pocket expense in the long run.

In Network:

Like snowflakes, not all networks are the same. For maternity care you want to make sure that the plan is "in-network" for your insurance plan. This little hack will make sure that the provider within your insurer's network will keep you from any out-of-network charges. By going to a health care provider that is absent from of the network, you'll incur two results: 1) If you are enrolled in a PPO you will have to cover the out-of-network rate and/or fine or 2) if you are enrolled in an HMO you will have to pay the entire bill. Think of it as losing the worst game of credit card roulette over a 9-month period. It is best to play it safe and double check your insurer's directory.

There are a plethora of variables to consider when planning the medical journey of your child's birth. Be it a traditional birth, via a surrogate or an adoption, the truth is that a doctor will be a vital member of your child's life and it is a decision that should not be taken lightly. Take your time to research everything from in-home births to hospital deliveries to vaccines and if and when to pierce your newborn's ears.

IN NEARLY ALL DEVELOPED COUNTRIES,
COMPREHENSIVE MATERNITY CARE IS FREE OR CHEAP FOR ALL.

THE IRISH EXAMPLE: **IRELAND ENSURES FREE MATERNITY CARE AT PUBLIC HOSPITALS, WHILE HAVING A PRIVATE DELIVERY OPTION AVAILABLE.**

THE AVERAGE PRICE **OF A NON-COMPLICATED** DELIVERY IS ROUGHLY $4,000 IN THE NETHERLANDS, WITH FRANCE AND SWITZERLAND AROUND $4,200.

THESE CHARGES ARE CONTROLLED WITH A COMBINATION OF REGULATION AND PRICE SETTING.

HOSPITAL VACAY! **THE $4,000 PRICE TAG** OFTEN INCLUDES THE 5 TO 7 RECOMMENDED HOSPITAL DAYS, **POST-BIRTH. THIS TIME IS SPENT HEALING** WHILE RELAXING WITH NEWBORN EDUCATIONAL CLASSES.

Average 2012 Amount Paid for Childbirth

		CONVENTIONAL DELIVERY	CAESAREAN
UNITED STATES	**$9,775**		**$15,041**
SWITZERLAND	$4,039		$5,186
FRANCE	$3,541		$6,441
CHILE	$2,992		$3,378
NETHERLANDS	$2,669		$5,328
BRITAIN	$2,641		$4,435
SOUTH AFRICA	$2,035		$3,449

Note: Amounts paid are the actual payments agreed to by insurance companies or other companies services, and are lower than billed charges. Amounts shown include routine prenatal, delivery, and postpartum obstetric care. Some care provided by practitioners other than obstetrician—like ultrasounds performed by a radiologist or blood testing by a lab—are not included in this tally.

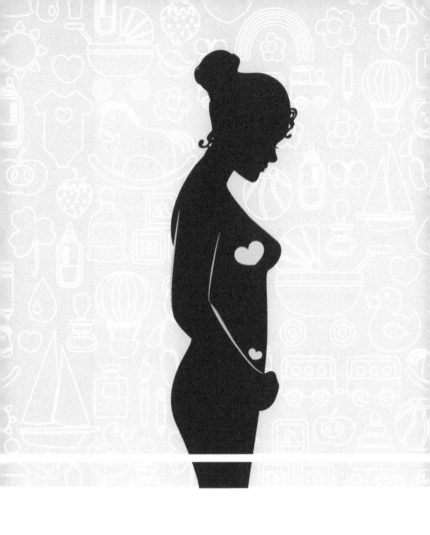

**You're Pregnant //
The First Trimester: How Exciting…and Scary**

The next nine months will go by faster than any other time period in your life. There will never be enough time to learn everything you want to know in order to feel like you are ready for a baby. The trick, however, is to stay excited. Never let the incredibly long "to do" list overwhelm the elation that your new family member will bring. This palpable excitement is a hack unto itself. By staying happy, you'll be able to keep a clear mind as you prepare everything to be as close to perfect as perfect can be.

A Hack for the Old Cliché: How to UNDERSTAND What to Expect When You're Expecting:

A pregnant body will constantly change, even very early on. While this is different in every woman, there are a few hints the body gives off that can help steer the pregnancy. Vibrant and sudden glitters of glow around the cheeks, shiny hair and soft gentle hands tend to be a positive sign that the mother is in great health, which is, of course, awesome for the baking bun, especially during those vital first three months of development. On the other hand, some women can feel absolutely horrible. So it's very important to keep track of these shifts. Here are some of the most common changes an expectant mother can expect, what these changes can mean, and which signs are red flags (spoiler alert, these are not going to be the most pleasant of symptoms).

Bloody Mary:

The numbers dictate that around a quarter of pregnant women will have slight bleeding during their first trimester. During these first stages of pregnancy, light spotting can be attributed to the fertilized embryo having implanted in the uterus. However, if you have a crime scene down there, stinging pain, and cramps, make sure to call your doctor. These may be signs of a miscarriage or an ectopic pregnancy (a pregnancy in which the embryo implants outside of the uterus).

Tenderizer:

Sore or tender breasts are generally the earliest sign that your family will be expanding. Tender breasts are a likely sign that your body is setting up your milk ducts to feed your baby. You may go up a bra size or more.

Constipation:

There's no other way to put it. It's going to happen. During pregnancy the muscle contractions that are usually responsible for moving food through the highway that is your intestines slow down due to inflated levels of the hormone progesterone. Think of this hormone like a construction crew taking up all three lanes and the median while you try to drive to work. A simple nutrient hack to 'keep the traffic moving' is to increase your fiber intake. Also, do not be tempted to eat chocolate, dairy products, red meat, bananas, and caffeine, as they will only add to your woes.

What the Heck is This?:

There is no need to be alarmed. Leukorrhea, more commonly known as discharge is a white ooze of sorts that you make experience early on during the first trimester. The only hack that can really be applied is to wear a panty liner which can help you feel more secure and comfortable. And never use a tampon as they can introduce germs into your baby's current home. If the ooze is followed by pain or discoloration, it is best to contact your doctor.

Damsel in Distress:

There is a lot going on in a pregnant body. Think of it as the human body constantly launching miniature fireworks of baby-developing goodness in all directions. This constant excess of hormones can take a large toll on the woman's body. Weakness, exhaustion, heavy eyes are just some of the more standard side effects of carrying a baby. The top hack to make sure you can survive the next nine months is to be well rested. Calcium and Iron supplements may be a close second.

Cravings?:

Yes and no. There's the old misconception that pregnant women will randomly want fried mushrooms with ice cream. Actually, we can guarantee some weirdness. The truth is your body's hormonal changes will affect your taste buds. So it is possible, and expected, that women will occasionally want churros or mangos with salt, and it's okay to give into these cravings from time to time, so long as the majority of your diet consists of healthy and balanced foods. Crazy enough, there is something to watch out for. It's called PICA --an extreme result of the changes that occur in the body. It's a craving of sorts where the pregnant woman will want to consume non-edible items like clay, soap and chalk among other things. Of course, this is ridiculously dangerous for both the mom and the baby.

Potty Training:

The growing baby and uterus are two roommates squeezing into the same dorm room. The result is pressure against the bladder which can result in unexpected flooding. By no means should eliminating or even reducing the liquid intake be considered in order to correct this. In fact, the only hack we recommend is to cut out coffee drinks, which stimulate the bladder and limit drinks around bedtime.

Heartburn:

There is so much going on in the body that it becomes difficult to know what is related to the pregnancy and what something else is. However, medical studies have shown that heartburn/acid reflux is something that will occur more frequently during pregnancy. It is perfectly normal, although many expectant mothers are unaware of this side effect and can perceive it as something more grim. To avoid this scare, expectant mothers should have smaller meals with limited grease, spices, and acidity.

Finally, a benefit for all the morning sickness, liquids and nausea...well, besides the baby. These super foods all offer up essential vitamins and minerals to ensure that the developing baby will be as healthy as possible.

Cereal as a Meal or Snack:

It will help from the first few weeks of pregnancy all the way to the delivery day. High in vitamin B, doctors and nutritionists suggest getting 400 micrograms per day through vitamin supplements or fortified foods, i.e., breakfast cereal. Most breakfast brands contain 400 micrograms per bowl. Just make sure you stay away from the sugar traps that are cereals marketed to kids. Add throughout the day vegetables like peas and asparagus, which are high in folate, and 400 micrograms will go down quickly.

Got Milk?:

There can't be a list that encourages the consumption of cereal without mentioning the benefits of milk. But there is no point of just having milk for the sake of having milk, right? So here's the logic behind the hack recommendation. A pregnant body will absorb somewhere around twice as much calcium from foods while it is supporting another life. Yet, a good majority of people constantly struggle to get an adequate amount of calcium in the first place. However, instead of just downing gallons of milk, try drinking nonfat milk. A simple 8-ounces of fat free milk will provide the body with 300 milligrams, or 30% of the 1,000 milligram suggested amount of calcium.

Bananas:

Fruits in general are a great way to incorporate tasty, sweet vitamins to a diet. For a growing baby, bananas are an excellent fruit to start with. *Honey, I Shrunk the Kids* taught us that these golden peel-friendly fruits offer a load of potassium and quick energy to fight off fatigue…and let's face it, pregnant women can always use more energy. Plus, bananas have been used for thousands of years to make nausea go away.

What?! No, Cheese?:

Get out of here! Cheese is the greatest thing to happen in life. You can't argue with cheese. It's just perfection. But doctors across the world suggest not having it while carrying a little one. But that's ludicrous. No one in their right mind would give up cheese for a baby. So how do you survive? Well, the hack is that only soft cheeses are off-limits. Hard cheeses like cheddar and mozzarella may not only help with your cheesy fix, but they also add calcium and protein to the diet. #teamcheese.

Galactic Salmon:

This high-quality protein is a remarkably good source of omega-3 fats, which help the baby develop. Also, omega-3 fats have been proven to improve a person's mood. Plus, swordfish, tilefish and other marine treats tend to be high in methylmercury, while salmon only has a small amount. That's key because a lot of methylmercury can be harmful to the baby's developing nervous system. To play it safe, never consume more than 12 ounces per week.

Fitness, Physical Health and Tai Chi

Safety First:

Finding a safe way to exercise that can be enjoyed while a baby forms inside can be difficult. Anyone can tell you it is safe to do pushups, lift weights, go rock climbing, but it is still nerve-wracking to try any of these high-intensity activities. Walking and swimming are the go-to work outs that expectant mothers flock to, but that's so mainstream.

If you want to be the hipster mom (and let's be honest, who doesn't want to be a hipster mom?), give a lighter form of martial arts, Tai Chi, a try. With its combination of fluid movements and deep breathing techniques, Tai Chi offers the entire mind, body, spirit, and energy workout that develops physical and mental strength while improving your balance and flexibility. Essentially, Tai Chi is very pregnant-friendly. By definition, it avoids all those uncomfortable, strenuous jerking motions that make working out with a developing body in you a little scary. Keep in mind that the main goal of Tai Chi is to help the circulation of positive energy throughout the body. In basic terms, think of this as a mix between peaceful meditation and yoga.

**You're Pregnant //
The Second Trimester: Prep Time**

reat news! You're not going to feel this weak for all nine months. There is a sunrise at the end of the first trimester. The science shows that during the second trimester those horrid mornings of fatigue and nausea and gooey stuff coming out of you are fading away. Between your body balancing out and the hacks we provided earlier, these next few months you'll be feeling like yourself again. With that in mind, this is the time to begin prepping your body and mind for the final push.

Getting Informed:

The second trimester begins on week 13 and runs through week 26. This is usually inaugurated with an ultrasound that can provide the baby's sex as well as a pretty cohesive update on their health. Also, while morning sickness may be a thing of the past, your body will still see some pretty major changes (no worries, we're covering 'pregnancy pants' next).

Back pain, headaches, and something called quickening are all part of the natural process. Some hacks to keep in mind are that you will gain weight and anytime that occurs, your body reacts differently. Expect some back pains and soreness to come along. Also, headaches and quickening are symptoms that tend to spark up during the second trimester.

Quickening is something that generally occurs around week 20 or so of the pregnancy ride. This exciting time is when you'll first be able to feel that there is someone inside of you. No need to freak out if it's week 21 and you haven't felt any baby move yet. Truth is, some women don't experience quickening until week 24 and beyond. It is just something to keep in mind as week 20 comes and goes.

Pregnancy Pants:

Your body is expanding. It's pretty exciting once you can start noticing the belly grow, but it can also be a stressful period as your wardrobe will appear inadequate. Add to that stress the fact that spending money on maternity wear might not be the best use of funds (you know, given that you're trying to save as much as possible now that the family budget includes one more). So what can you do? Here are some of the wardrobe tips, tricks and hacks to simplify the hassle of standing in front of the mirror on a Monday morning.

Jean Life Extension:

You can quickly and easily add an inch to your favorite jeans with a button extender. The product does just what the name promises and for a fraction of the price of brand new jeans. If you are feeling a bit crafty you can attempt to make your own extension using twist-ties, rubber bands or shoe strings. Simply unbutton the jeans, wrap the string around the button and simply tie at the other end.

Double Sided Tape:

Button-down shirts are usually a nightmare for women with larger busts. As it turns out, breasts tend to grow (quite a bit) as the pregnancy carries on. Applying double-sided tape to the inside of any button-down shirt makes it a flexible, comfortable and safe clothing option. A light cami underneath is another inexpensive way to feel comfortable as you dress for two.

Giving In:

It's bound to happen. You can fight it, hack it with rubber bands, strings and your partner's XXL college t-shirt, but eventually the maternity aisle will call your name. Before heading over to the department stores, consider the consignment stores. They tend to have a wide selection of gently-used items that may be fairly trendy.

While shopping, keep in mind that most sizes are measured against your pre-pregnancy size. If you're unsure of the size, play it safe and go larger over snug.

Fabrics like nylon, Lycra, and cotton jersey are meant to be stretchy. These are by far the best materials to invest in as you can carry them throughout most of the pregnancy.

Temperature will play a big role when it comes to the comfort you experience while pregnant as hormones teeter and totter. During the second trimester the body adjusts to the internal changes by spiking in temperature. From very hot to severely cold, there will rarely be a time when your body will feel at ease. A simple way to combat this discomfort is to apply layers to your wardrobe for easy air control.

Fake bellies are prosthetic add-ons that most maternity stores carry. You can simply slide it on at the store and test out a few articles to assure yourself that what you buy will fit later on.

Staying Active

The general consensus is that the more active you are the healthier you feel. However, an expectant mother can have reservations about doing intense training with a baby in her. The key factor is to keep your body moving in a safe and enjoyable manner. Countless studies have shown that pregnant women who exercise tend to incur less back pain, have more energy, and have a faster return to their pre-pregnancy shape.

Yet, making time, paying for a membership, and most importantly, finding the energy to work out is always easier said than done. But we wouldn't be the hack kings if we didn't have simple, inexpensive solutions that meet nearly everyone's needs.

Here are our **TOP 3** home routines that are easy on the body, not too time-consuming and best of all, reputedly safe to perform during any stages of pregnancy.

Ballet Plié Squats:

This first move comes from the classically trained world of ballet. Simply stand parallel to the back of a chair. Making sure the chair is set up to be sturdy with good balance. Using the hand closest to the chair for balance, bring your feet parallel while keeping them hip-distance apart.

Then easily turn your toes and knees out to 45 degrees, while pulling your belly button up and in. Now bend your knees, having your torso go as low as possible while your back remains straight. Then return to the original position by straightening your legs. This movement will strengthen your quadriceps, hamstrings and butt while increasing your natural balance.

Scissor Thighs:

While resting on your right side, provide support to your head using your arm. Then with the right leg bent at a 45-degree angle and left leg straight, bring your opposite arm onto the floor. Now simply lift your left leg to a little over your hip height and repeat. Afterwards bend your left knee and place it on top of foam or pillows for added support. Flex open your right leg and lift it as high as possible. Finally, switch sides and repeat. This movement will increase strength and flexibility in your core and thighs.

Planking for 9 Months:

Start by getting down on your hands and knees on a foamed and comfortable yoga mat. Make sure your wrists are directly under your shoulders. Once you are in the position, lift your knees and straighten your legs behind you until your body forms a straight line. Try to avoid arching your back as much as possible. Also, keep your belly as tight as possible. Maintain this for a count of 5 to 10 breaths. Doing it correctly for the duration of your pregnancy will increase your breathing while strengthening your core and arms.

The Ultimate Guide
for
EXCERCISING
DURING PREGNANCY

Second trimester
13 to 28 weeks

4 5 6

Tip: **AT THIS POINT** IN YOUR PREGNANCY, IT'S A GOOD IDEA TO **STOP LYING ON YOUR BACK.**

Your growing uterus can start to push down on some of your major blood vessels, restricting your blood flow.

CAUTION:
To avoid this, stay away from any stretches and exercises that require you lay flat, and try to stop sleeping on your back as well.

 Tip: **STAY HYDRATED.**

A pregnant woman should drink between **2 & 3 liters of fluid daily**, and needs an extra cup for each hour of excercise.

Try to **avoid caffiene**, and definitely **don't drink any alcohol!**

Tip: AS YOUR BELLY GROWS, YOU WILL FIND YOURSELF OFF BALANCE AT TIMES.

Make sure that you avoid situtations where you could easily fall and injure yourself.

Wearing high heels may become dangerous, and so can other daily activities. Use extra caution as your belly gets bigger.

Start Keeping Track of Everything:

In general, the second trimester is widely accepted as the most manageable trimester. The initial shock of joy, fear and excitement has subsided (a bit) and you now find yourself looking at strollers, preparing a nursery and even considering names. Because this time can be very hectic, it becomes easy to lose track of the small things.

The Hack Here is More of a Suggestion:

Plan, plan, and plan some more. During the second trimester the delivery day can seem like a lifetime away. Yet, you should be prepared for the unexpected. Have a suitcase pre-packed by your bedroom door. You can also have a backup suitcase in your car in the event that your water breaks while you're not home. Have emergency contacts ready. Whether it is your parents, your partner, or your close friend, let them know an approximate delivery date so that they can coordinate work and life schedules.

You're Pregnant //
The Third Trimester: Brace Yourself,
Childbirth is Coming

Just around the corner lies the biggest thing to happen in your life since Starbucks introduced the Pumpkin Spice Latte. With just a few more weeks to plan for, this final haul can seem a bit overwhelming. Between time management, budgeting and the ever-growing fear that 'whoa, this is actually happening,' it is easy to see how you can feel trapped in a whirlwind of highs and lows.

Final Physical

The Braxton Hicks Contractions:

Sounds like a funky alternative band so indie they're not even on Pandora. But in reality they are just mild contractions. These contractions serve as warm-ups to prepare the uterus for the main event. Braxton Hicks contractions tend to be calmer than the actual labor contractions. As you get closer and closer to the delivery week, the contractions will begin to resemble labor contractions – but even then, the discomfort will not be the same. The biggest difference is that actual contractions start to get closer and more intense while the Braxton Hicks variety are fairly consistent.

More of the Uncomfortable Stuff:

From backaches and bleeding to discharges and, yes, hemorrhoids, the last few weeks will definitely be a physical test. Fatigue will be the umbrella term that encompasses all these discomforts. The extra weight, the lack of sleep, and the constant need to pee all wear you out. But you can make small adjustments to help provide more energy and comfort. For starters, the early hacks on diet and exercise are a great way to keep your body going. Taking naps can also add a nice little boost of natural energy. And when all else fails, just sit down, relax, and take a few minutes to do a whole lot of nothing. Anything you can do to be relaxed, happy and at peace will really make the delivery that much easier.

Warning Signs:

The little bundle of joy is almost here, so let's quickly review to make sure everything will come out perfectly.

Call your Doctor Immediately:

If any of the following symptoms appear. There is just no sense in playing it cautious with your baby and your health.

      i.   Severe abdominal pain or cramps

      ii. Severe nausea or vomiting

      iii. Bleeding

      iv. Severe dizziness

      v. Pain or burning during urination

      vi. Rapid weight gain (more than 6.5 pounds per month) or too little weight gain

Weeks 1-2:

The **fertilization** occurs
& the 'implantation' triggers
hormonal and physical
changes in your body.

(*Weeks* 1-12)

Weeks 13-18:

The fetus starts sprouting hair, developing eyesight
and eyelashes. If the woman carrying the baby has
been pregnant before, she might notice some
movement around this time but the first-timers
usually notice movements later. By this time,
pregnancy discomforts women experience have
toned down and are less noticeable.

(*Weeks* 13-28)

Weeks 29-33:

The women start lactating around
these weeks. The baby is consider-
ably getting bigger every week and
the baby's brain is developing rapidly.
The baby has developed hearing and
now can respond to stimuli.

(*Weeks* 29-40)

Weeks 3-8:

These weeks are called the embryonic stage, during which the embryo develops the major and vital organs. Which is why the baby is really vulnerable during this time period. The women also experience a lot of discomfort for these first few months because they are going through many hormonal and physical changes.

Weeks 9-12:

By the ninth week, the baby is a little more than an inch long and it is now called a fetus. By now the woman's uterus has grown from the size of the fist to about the size of a grapefruit. The baby also builds bone, muscle, and cartilage during these weeks.

Weeks 19-23:

The baby's skin now has a protective coating to protect it from the amniotic fluid. You can determine the gender of the baby by week 20. By week 23, most women can notice the Linea Nigra on their stomach. It is a dark line running from the belly button to the pubic bone.

Weeks 24-28:

The baby is developing body fat around this time, the facial features are more developed, and the pregnant woman's belly button may have popped out. By week 26, your baby opens his/her eyes and by week 28, your baby starts blinking and dreaming!

Weeks 34-37:

The baby's brain is still developing but most of the other vital organs are fully developed. Also the lungs are not completely developed yet.

Weeks 38-40/42:

Now the baby is ready to be born, the lungs are developed, your baby can fully respond to stimuli, blink, and hear. By the end of the pregnancy, most babies change position and turn their heads towards the pelvis.

18-20 inches

7lbs

PREGNANCY IS DIFFERENT FOR EVERY WOMAN, FOR SOME IT LASTS TILL 40 WEEKS, FOR SOME IT LASTS LESS, AND FOR SOME IT MAY EVEN LAST 42 WEEKS! BY THE END OF THE PREGNANCY, THE AVERAGE BABY WEIGHS ABOUT 7 POUNDS AND IS ABOUT 18-20 INCHES LONG.

Out of the Box Thinking

Dream Journal:

Peculiar dreams come in bulk during pregnancy. Most doctors agree it probably has something to do with the hormonal imbalance going on in your system. Whatever the reason, prepare to have some pretty obscure and memorable dreams. A creative way to have fun with these is to start a dream journal where you record your dreams in as much detail as possible. You can then give the journal to your child on a momentous occasion.

Herbal Baby:

There are blurred lines and skewed opinions on herbs and pregnancy. The scientific community tends to stay clear from them because of the lack of scientific studies. University studies have shown that it's safe to eat low to moderate amounts of fresh or dried herbs in cooked meals with the exception to the rule being sage, due to its correlation to high blood pressure. Of course, always check with your doctor before taking any remedies. The University of Maryland's Medical Center notes that herbs contain chemicals that may cross into the placenta to your baby.

Acupuncture:

University studies have looked into this physical remedy as a cure for any and all of the negative feels symptoms associated with carrying a baby. The shocking news is that acupuncture appears to be a fairly effective way to limit depression symptoms during pregnancy. Now this result was from only one study done by Stanford University, but we would be hard-pressed to not include a hack that could potentially help with prenatal depression.

HERBAL REMEDY	REASON FOR CAUTION IN PREGNANCY

Chamomile

May cause irritation and allergic reactions when used as a cream on the skin.

Excessive use may cause stimulation of the nervous system and insomnia.

Eucalyptus

Safe as a diluted essential oil in small doses, and can be added to steam inhalation to relieve sinuses.

ONLY USE FOR SHORT PERIODS.
Undiluted oil on your skin may cause irritation.

DON'T INGEST the essential oil, as this can cause gastric upset.

Ginger

Large amounts may cause blood thinning, so avoid if you have a history of miscarriage or any vaginal bleeding during this pregnancy. Excessive amounts may cause abdominal discomfort, heartburn and skin itching. Don't exceed about three teaspoons of grated root ginger a day.

Stop taking ginger at least two weeks before any planned surgery, including caesarean.

Lavender

DO NOT use if you are taking drugs for heart complaints or antacid medication for heartburn.

Peppermint

May cause heartburn, nausea, vomiting and allergic reactions, including skin irritation, when the oil is used on skin. May be a heart stimulant.

DO NOT use if you are taking drugs for heart complaints or antacid medication for heartburn.

CHAPTER 2 //
CUTENESS APLENTY

**You're Pregnant //
Congratulations! It's A…**

G iving Birth - We should slow down...before we get to cutting the umbilical cord, let's hack away at all the different options that exist in this 21st century delivery room.

Traditional Birth is the vaginal childbirth that allows the baby to pass through the birth canal.

Cesarean Birth (C-Section) can be part of a pregnancy plan, but is usually seen as an emergency procedure in order to guarantee the safest delivery for the baby.

Midwife Birth involves a midwife, or personal care provider, for an expectant mom. Some are certified nurse practitioners. A midwife will work with you and the medical team before, during and after childbirth.

Doula Birth involves a doula, or birth assistant. Some have specialized training. They navigate through labor with a calming ambiance of relaxation and breathing exercises, massages, words of encouragement and anything else that will make you feel at ease.

Water Birth is just like it sounds – you give birth while in a tube of sorts. Now, it's not for everyone as water births require particular criteria, a consent form, and a pre-birth walkthrough.

Surrogate Birth is a modern advancement to help families have a child when the mother cannot carry the baby. The surrogate woman becomes pregnant using a type of assisted reproductive technology, most commonly done via IVF. As a result she will become pregnant and nurse the baby to term, gives birth, and then turn the baby over to the hospital and parents.

Adoption 101

State regulations differ depending on which side of the Mississippi you are on as well as what year you are reading this. The world of adoption is constantly evolving. Adoption should be as wonderful an experience as possible for both the child being adopted and the new parents, but it has become progressively more complex. To simplify this topic (because it's what we like to do), we've broken adoption down into the seven most common steps that are usually associated with the process.

The Decision:

Duh, the first step is deciding that you want to adopt. Whatever the reason is, there are countless foster kids across the globe praying for a family, so on their behalf: thank you. Once you've decided to adopt, you'll want to contact your local adoption agency and attend an orientation meeting.

Paper Work:

Unlike the conventional baby-making process, adopting comes with a lot more paperwork. You'll want to wrap up all the required training and your application to adopt as soon as possible as it can be a slow process.

Inspection:

The next step to look forward to is the home study. Basically the case worker who you've been working with will drop by your home to determine if you are ready to look after a child.

Approved!

While the home inspection is taking place, all the forms and background checks from step two are being processed. Shortly after you ace the home inspection you can expect one of the happiest phone calls of your life.

Match Maker:

Being paired with a child is the fifth step. All things will be considered during this step: from the child's needs, personality and if he or she has siblings.

Placement:

Preparing for an adoptive placement is one of the final steps in the adoption process. It generally happens after a potential match has been located and agreed upon by you, the caseworker, and the child's caseworker.

Welcome Home!

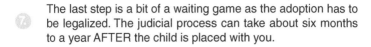

The last step is a bit of a waiting game as the adoption has to be legalized. The judicial process can take about six months to a year AFTER the child is placed with you.

Adopting internationally has this daunting aura hanging over it, and it is easy to see why. Anything that deals with borders tends to be a headache. Yet, that couldn't be further from the truth. There are countless organizations across the US and other developed countries, that make the international adoption process a joyous occasion. However, those regulations change constantly. And per region. After conducting some pretty intensive research there are a few places to get started. Adoption.com has a 40 slide power point on their site that breaks down anything and everything related to the experience in the international adoption process. The World Child Organization also has some great material into adopting internationally and their twitter account is highly active, making it a breeze to stay current with the latest regulations.

Check them out: @KidsFirstAdoption

GAVIN JACKSON HARPER
HENRY EVAN GABRIEL CHRISTIAN
ISAAC HANNAH RILEYY ALEXIS CARTER EVELYN ELLA
NATALIE LANDON AUDREY BENJAMIN DANIEL
SOPHIA HAILEY CHRISTOPHER MICHAEL
LUKE JORDAN
JAYDEN GABRIELLA CAMILA EMMA
ELIZABETH LAYLA AALIYAH
ELIJAH SAMUEL CALEB MIA
JOSEPH WILLIAM NEVAEH KAYLEE
GRACE ZOE OLIVIA MASON DAVID
ETHAN SARAH AVA CHLOE LILY ELI SAMANTHA
ASHLEY LIAM
ISABELLA SOFIA ADDISON ARIANNA
ALLISON JAMES MATTHEW
MADISON NOAH AUBREY DYLAN AVERY
ANNA CLAIRE TAYLOR ALYSSA JACK
LUCAS JONATHAN ANTHONY CHARLOTTE
WYATT BROOKLYN JOSHUA LILLIAN RYAN
HUNTER ANDREW LOGAN
BRAYDEN NICHOLAS
VICTORIA LEAH NATHAN
ALEXANDER
ISAIAH TYLER SAVANNAH
AIDEN OWEN
AMELIA
ABIGAIL ZOEY
JOHN EMILY
JACOB

**HOW
SHALL WE
NAME THE
BABY?**

**Cuteness Aplenty //
Naming Rights**

This is a tough one. The name you pick for your child will stick with them, well, forever. Names, like food trends tend to be fairly cyclical. The staples like mac and cheese, pizza and cake are always popular while kale, quail and gluten-free free-roaming turkey bacon have their highs and lows. But the truth is, none of that should matter. Some people, like my mom for instance, had names picked out decades in advance, while other people are hit with sudden bolts of inspiration at the most obscure time. Here are a few hacks to consider when selecting the name of your child.

Name with your Heart

Make a Short List:

Consider relatives, friends, heroes, and memories. Anyone you would like to pay tribute to.

Share the Bad Ones:

Pick names you don't like and run them by friends and family. If they like any of the bad names, cross them off the list when you are ready to get opinions on the final few. Those who were honest with you and agreed with the names you didn't like probably share some like-thinking with you, making them ideal for bouncing name ideas with.

Say the Name Out Loud:

Name plants, goldfish, and anything else around your home with nicknames associated to that name. Do you like how it sounds? Consider that your baby's friends will probably employee these nicknames.

Write it Down:

One thing is saying it and pronouncing it a thousand different ways. But when you see it on a piece of white paper followed by your last name, it's magical. Definitely a nice little hack to consider if you are stuck between a few names.

Middle Names:

 Why not? They are becoming increasingly popular across the country and it gives your child options if they feel that they don't identify with their name.

The Smile Test:

 A great way to help you decide if you're stuck is to keep those names on you at all times. Whenever you come across some bad news or if you're just having an overall bad day, look at the names. If there is a name that makes you smile more than the others, pick it.

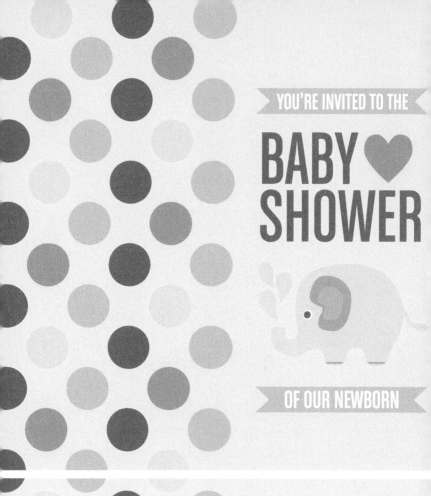

YOU'RE INVITED TO THE

BABY ♥ SHOWER

OF OUR NEWBORN

**Cuteness Aplenty //
Baby Shower**

Your first baby shower is a completely new experience. Whether you've been planning the baby for a long time, or it was an unexpected surprise, or you just got approval for your adoption, a baby shower is something all new parents should experience. It's also the last party you'll ever have where your kid won't be on the guest list. There are endless ways to transform the baby shower from a simple backyard Sunday gift exchange to a memorable celebration of a growing family. Here's our collection of the best hacks for a memorable shower!

Think Themes:

Whether you're throwing your own shower or it's the future godparents hosting it, a themed party is a no-brainer. From *Goodnight Moon* to *Harry Potter* to a French Café, implementing a theme helps the shower stand out from the rest.

Interactive Games:

Games that have everyone participating will help break the ice for those guests who do not know everyone. A personal favorite is the guess the baby guest. Simply ask each invitee to bring a snapshot of themselves as a baby. Pin the pictures up and have guests guess which baby is which guest.

A Snazzy Affair:

Using beautifully designed glass decanters for drinks is an easy and inexpensive way to step up the display while adding a touch of sophistication to the party.

Gender Surprise:

While most guests would prefer to know the baby's gender before buying a gift, that can't always be the case. You can use the shower to get creative and reveal the gender by incorporating blue or pink to certain aspects of the party (i.e., the cake, drinks or your outfit).

Bored Jar and Bibs:

A DIY event that pays off months and even years after the shower is the Bored Jar and Bibs table. At the shower set up a small table with a Mason jar labeled: bored. Ask the guests to write down simple solutions to the inevitable "I'm bored" day. On the same table lay out standard white bibs that guests can decorate with paint, glitter and any other crafty supplies you would like to include.

Cuteness Aplenty //
Mensa Baby

It's something we all want and something we can all benefit from: genius babies! Just imagine giant-headed babies floating telepathically as they launch mankind towards a new horizon. Well, maybe not that extreme, but still, there are ways to help develop your child's mind. Experts across the world agree that Infant-development in the first twelve months is crucial. During the first year of life, the baby's mind is prime for learning, so here are the brain hacks to help them reach their full potential.

Brain Games

Stimulating the Eyes:

Setting up the foundation for letter and number recognition can be done by holding up two pictures roughly 10 to 12 inches away from their cute little faces. The images should be similar with a single noticeable difference; like one with a parent holding an iPad and one with the parent holding a mango instead. Your little infant will go back and forth trying to distinguish the difference, prepping the mind for letter recognition down the line.

Tickle Monster:

Any excuse to play with your new baby is a great excuse. But this one has great benefits. Giggling caused by gentle tickling is the first step in developing a sense of humor. On that same note, games like "This little piggy," and "I'm going to get you" help the baby comprehend anticipation.

The Narration Game:

While we are on the subject of anticipation, try narrating small, repetitive activities like lunch time or changings. Your baby will pick up on the routines and repeating the same words over a period of time will begin to trigger associations in the baby's mind.

Topsy Turvy:

Imagine eating breakfast, lunch and dinner every day from the exact same spot. Seems kind of silly. Well, your baby thinks so, too. Give switching their high chair's location a try. From eating on the other side of the table to enjoying a meal on the balcony, this change of scenery helps memory and location development.

Texture Test:

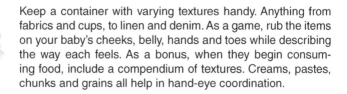

Keep a container with varying textures handy. Anything from fabrics and cups, to linen and denim. As a game, rub the items on your baby's cheeks, belly, hands and toes while describing the way each feels. As a bonus, when they begin consuming food, include a compendium of textures. Creams, pastes, chunks and grains all help in hand-eye coordination.

Besides these tidbits, things like exposing your baby to art, music and life in general seems like an ideal way to not just help the brain, but create lifelong family memories. The truth is that no one can guarantee a 157 I.Q., but that shouldn't be the goal. Simply focus on cherishing these times and doing anything and everything you think will make your baby happier and healthier.

**Cuteness Aplenty //
Exhausted Yet?**

It's hard enough to balance a career and/or an education, a social life and your health before you have a baby, but hey, what the heck, why not juggle one more thing....oh boy. It's okay, we have some simple hacks to make this circus act a little easier to manage.

Career Help:

If you're lucky enough to work at an office space with a day care, congrats. Take advantage of it. But if that's not an option, consider working from home. And when that idea gets rejected, consider the new and scary. Consider this the perfect time to quit that awful 9-5 that you hate and try your hand at the entrepreneurial world of Etsy or opening up your own coffee shop. You know, those dreams you had before corporate America and the mighty dollar showed up. Finances with a new baby are always scary, but so is the idea of dragging yourself to the same job you hate for forty years while your baby is raised by babysitters, grandparents and afterschool baseball, tennis and karate. A career change to a more flexible market might seem like an insane idea, but it might also be the best thing to ever happen to you (besides the bundle of joy this book focuses on).

Friends:

Your phone can really help you stay connected. But if you want to actually participate in life, make sure you follow up on missed texts and calls. Everyone will understand if you don't answer your phone right after you bring your new kid home. But if you have a few minutes between naps and dinner, make sure to text back. This small social interaction will lead to making plans and keeping you young.

Gym:

Speaking of staying young. Let's be honest. Going to the gym while having a new love in your life, come on. There's no need to lie to you here with makeshift ways to coordinate your schedule with nine other people so that there is always someone watching the baby as you head towards the gym. The fact is you had a baby for a reason, enjoy it. Take the baby with you on your fitness ventures. Stroll through the park, do some yoga in the backyard as your newborn naps underneath a tree, instead of driving your baby around at night to get them to sleep, take them out to the backyard to watch you plank, push up and sit up. This stimulation will allow your baby to concentrate on you which should calm them down before bed time.

MISTAKES TO AVOID

LET YOUR BABY – **CRY**

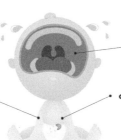

• COMMUNICATION

HELPS *in* MUSCLE DEVELOPMENT.

Lung DEVELOPMENT

OVER AND
UNDER FEEDING

MOST NEWBORNS NEED
8-12 FEEDINGS A DAY

SIGNS OF A HUNGRY BABY =
STIRRING, RESTLESSNESS,
SUCKING MOTIONS AND LIP MOVEMENTS.

THE MAJORITY OF NEWBORNS
LOSE WEIGHT AFTER BIRTH.

TAKES 10 – 14 DAYS TO
REGAIN THIS WEIGHT.
COULD BE AS MUCH AS 21 DAYS.

SAFETY FIRST

USE A **CAR SEAT** –
REDUCE RISK TO
INFANTS BY **71%**
AND **TODDLERS** BY **54%**

BOOSTER SEATS REDUCE
THE RISK OF SERIOUS
INJURY BY **45%**

Baby On Board

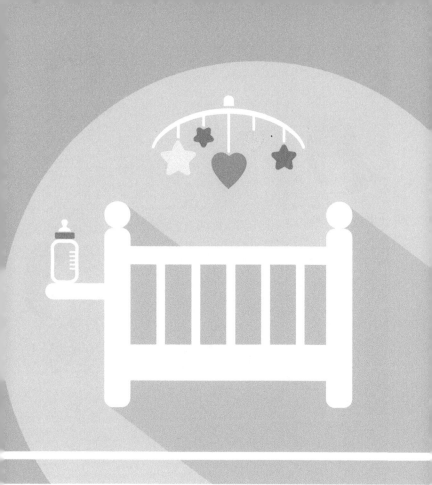

CHAPTER 3 //
Feeding and Sleeping

BREASTFEEDING
POSITIONS

Cross-Cradle

Cradle

Side-Lying

Football

Feeding and Sleeping //
Breast Feeding

It's become somewhat of a social movement as more and more studies justify its nutritional value. Yet, it is still somewhat of a taboo subject, in particular when speaking about breastfeeding in public. So what's our hack? Well, we have quick and easy solutions to how, when, where and why to breastfeed. So let's get started.

The Benefits:

The obvious benefits lie in the milk's rich nutrients and antibodies, which help your baby fight infections while at the same time create defenses against allergies. However, there are other trends that point to breastfeeding as the basis for life-long health. Studies have shown that kids who are breastfed are less likely to become overweight, develop diabetes, or get childhood leukemia later in life. Beyond benefits for the child, breastfeeding has a pretty great upside for the parents. Interestingly enough, research suggests that women who breast-feed tend to have lower risks of type 2 diabetes, breast cancer, ovarian cancer, high blood pressure, and heart disease.

A Brand New Experience:

All breastfeeding should begin with freshly washed hands. Let's just try to stay as sanitary as possible. As your baby is feeding away, you may be concerned that they can't breathe. However, you should know that the nostrils of an infant are set to allow air in and out while they are eating. Even so, if you are nervous, feel free to press down on your breast to allow for an easier flow of air.

Hacks for Getting Started

For a first time mother, just the notion of breastfeeding may seem somewhat foreign. To make this natural process a little more comfortable, consider these tips.

Positioning:

Try to get as relaxed as possible. Ideally, you want a position where you will not be moving around too much. There is litera-ture aplenty which suggests that mothers should breastfeed in a reclined position, about 45 degrees or so, especially during the first few weeks of feeding. This angle also enables gravity to help in the support of the baby while he or she is still at an ideal position to eat.

First Memory Together:

The earlier you start the feeding process, the better. Skin to skin contact is like a trigger for a newborn to feel at ease. So if you can get to breastfeeding quickly, this will train them to associate you with comfort and happiness. This will also add to the baby's abilities to latch on, making the process easier for both of you.

Signs of a Good Meal:

The most common concern for first time mothers is whether or not the baby ate well, enough, too much, etc. A good hack for testing this is to know if your baby is latched on well. A healthy feeding is triggered when you feel a gentle tugging sensation on your breast. Next you'll want to check to make sure your newborn is swallowing. The temple and lower jaw will move metrically with an occasional exhaling sound, which is your baby confirming that she swallowed.

Avoiding the Soreness

There are a few hacks you can apply in order to reduce the chance of soreness and discomfort post-feeding.

1. If the sucking action causes physical pain, that is most likely a sign that the baby is not in the correct positon.

2. Try switching breasts between meals. Always start with the one that feels less sore.

3. Wash your nipples daily with warm water. Staying away from soaps and lotion that may contain alcohol is also suggested.

4. Some women rub lanolin on their nipples in order to soothe them.

5. Stay away from bra pads lined with plastic and make sure to change bra pads between feedings to stay dry.

Not all women can breastfeed. Sometimes it's a biological thing, others it can just not feel natural. Whatever your reasons for not breastfeeding, don't drive yourself mad over it. Health, intense discomfort, or frustration can all lead to you second-guessing yourself and there is no need to. While experts agree that breastfeeding is the best nutritional option for babies, it's not the end-all-be-all. Truth is, well-researched commercial formulas are nutritious and even contain some vitamins and nutrients that breastfed babies need to get from supplements.

Feeding and Sleeping //
What to Eat and What to Avoid

WHAT TO EAT & WHAT TO AVOID

PLETHORA OF VEGGIES & FRUITS.

SEAFOOD (KEEP AN EYE ON YOUR MERCURY CONSUMPTION),

LEAN MEATS & POULTRY.

EGGS, BEANS, AND NUTS.

FAT-FREE MILK.

BROWN RICE, 100% WHOLE-WHEAT BREAD & FORTIFIED CEREALS.

FISH & SHELLFISH NUTRIENTS

HAT HELP A CHILD'S YES AND MIND.

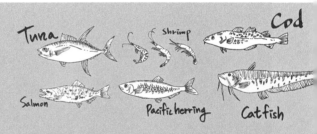

T SEAFOOD 2 OR 3 DAYS A WEEK. MIX & MATCH FROM A COLLECTION OF THE SEA: SALMON, TFISH, COD, HERRING, SHRIMP, CANNED LIGHT TUNA (NO MORE THAN 6 OUNCES A WEEK).

TAY AWAY FROM
SH WITH LOTS OF
MERCURY

WORDFISH, TILEFISH,
ARK, & KING MACKEREL.

TRY DRINKING A GLASS OF WATER
OR A GLASS OF FAT-FREE MILK
EVERY TIME YOU BREASTFEED.

LIMIT OR AVOID DRINKS THAT ARE HIGH IN CAFFEINE OR ADDED SUGARS.

Alcohol?!

If you must, wait until your baby is at least 4 months old. Drink only in moderation. The recommended is NO MORE than 1 drink a day. And plan, plan, plan! If and when your baby gets hungry outside of the normal routine, ALWAYS pump some breast milk before having any alcohol. Wait a minimum of 5 hours after having a drink before breastfeeding.

Solid Foods:

Babies are like computers, when they are ready for an update they'll tell you. One sign that your little one is ready for solid food is in its head control. Once they can keep their head in a steady upright position, it might be time to introduce solids.

The 'Extrusion Reflex' is a defense mechanism when your tongue shoves food out of your mouth. Babies come equipped with this feature, but they lose it right around the same time their heads start to self-balance. The ending of the reflex tends to be a pretty good barometer of when to introduce solids.

Weight gain and time are two of the more traditional indicators that a baby is ready for real food. Keep track of when they have doubled their birth weight, or weigh somewhere around 15 pounds and are at least 4 months old.

**Feeding and Sleeping //
Teething Pains**

Drooling:

Teething stimulates drooling. This can begin as early as 10 weeks into their adorable life and run up to 3 or 4 months of age.

Teething Rash:

Excess drool leads to dripping that can cause chafing on your little ones chin and neck. Check for redness and rashes around the mouth for early signs.

Vaseline can be used to set up a shield. Nipple cream also works as it is great for protecting the soft baby skin.

Coughing and Gagging:

Another sign that your baby is drooling too much is a light cough. Monitor it to make sure it is not a cold.

Nibbling:

The discomfort of the teeth breaking out is combatted naturally by the body through biting. This counter pressure makes the pain less severe.

Teething Diet:

For some babies the discomfort and pain is so severe that they simply will not eat. This can be a problem, so it is best to keep at it. After all, you are the parent.

Refusal to Feed:

Uncomfortable, cranky babies yearn to be soothed by something in their mouths — whether a bottle or the breast.

Facial Expressions:

Teething babies tend to tug irately at their ear or rub their cheek or chin. It's pretty simple as to why they do this: the gums, ears and cheeks share nerve pathways, so when your gums hurt, your cheeks and ears can ache as well.

While teething is unavoidable, you can help take it away with these baby-tested remedies:

Chewing:

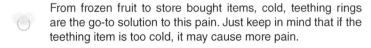

From frozen fruit to store bought items, cold, teething rings are the go-to solution to this pain. Just keep in mind that if the teething item is too cold, it may cause more pain.

Counter Pressure:

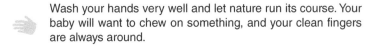

Wash your hands very well and let nature run its course. Your baby will want to chew on something, and your clean fingers are always around.

Pain Relief:

When chewing, rubbing and sucking frost foods don't work, use some good old fashioned acetaminophen…just make sure to keep your doctor in the loop.

**Feeding and Sleeping //
Zzz…**

A new parent's dream. Getting a baby to sleep for an extended period of time is about as hard as picking a TV series to binge watch on Netflix. But with proper game planning it can be accomplished.

Point of Exhaustion:

Something that can be difficult with a newborn, but fairly easy with a toddler. Between outdoor games, indoor cleaning and a bath, tuckering out a little one can seem like a full time job. But if managed correctly, this can lead to an exhausted child napping for quite some time. Now if you have a newborn at home, you can get creative in ways to encourage sleep. Placing them on a rolling walker and letting them move around is a great first-step. Swings and games are also a couple of other ways to get your baby to run out of energy.

Spanish Style:

From Barcelona to Bogota, in Spanish culture, naps are a big deal. Traditionally, babies and toddlers are provided with a hefty lunch around noon or so and then it's off to bed. This can be a great change of pace if you're having a difficult time getting your baby to relax during the day.

Temperature Control:

We all have that ideal sleep temperature. Whether it is a freezing room with three blankets or a warmer ambiance without socks. Babies are the same. Study your little one and see what the room feels like when they fall asleep quicker compared to the times when they struggle to rest.

Sleep Requirements

SCIENTIFIC STUDY OF 493 KIDS OVER A 16 YEAR PERIOD

1 *Month old:*

THE AVERAGE BABY
SLEPT 14-15 HOURS A DAY

50%
OF BABIES
GOT BETWEEN
13 & 16 HOURS

96%
OF BABIES
GOT BETWEEN
9 & 19 HOURS

3 *Month old:*

THE AVERAGE BABY
SLEPT 14-15 HOURS A DAY

50%
OF BABIES
GOT BETWEEN
13 & 16 HOURS

96%
OF BABIES
GOT BETWEEN
10 & 19 HOURS

6 *Month old:*

THE AVERAGE BAB
SLEPT 14 HOURS A DA

50%
OF BABIES
GOT BETWEEN
13 & 15.5 HOUR

96%
OF BABIES
GOT BETWEEN
10.5 & 18 HOUR

9 *Month old:*

THE AVERAGE BABY
SLEPT 13 HOURS A DAY

50%
OF BABIES
GOT BETWEEN
13 & 15 HOURS

96%
OF BABIES
GOT BETWEEN
10.5 & 17 HOURS

1 *Year old:*

THE AVERAGE BABY
SLEPT 13 HOURS A DAY

50%
OF BABIES
GOT BETWEEN
13 & 14 HOURS

96%
OF BABIES
GOT BETWEEN
11 & 16.5 HOURS

18 *Months old:*

THE AVERAGE BABY
SLEPT 13 HOURS A DA

50%
OF BABIES
GOT BETWEEN
12 & 14 HOURS

96%
OF BABIES
GOT BETWEEN
11 & 16 HOURS

2 *Years old:*

THE AVERAGE BABY
SLEPT 13 HOURS A DAY

50%
OF BABIES
GOT BETWEEN
12 & 14 HOURS

96%
OF BABIES
GOT BETWEEN
10 & 15.5 HOURS

THESE NUMBERS REPRESENT TOTAL SLEEP
DURATION—HOW MUCH BABIES SLEPT OVER
24-HOUR PERIOD. OF COURSE, NOT ALL OF TH
SLEEP TIME OCCURRED AT NIGHT.

Nap Time

Month old:

HE AVERAGE BABY
APPED 5-6 HOURS A DAY

50%
OF BABIES
NAPPED BETWEEN
4.5 & 7 HOURS

96%
OF BABIES
NAPPED BETWEEN
2 & 9 HOURS

3 Month old:

THE AVERAGE BABY
NAPPED 5 HOURS A DAY

50%
OF BABIES
GOT BETWEEN
3 & 6 HOURS

96%
OF BABIES
GOT BETWEEN
1 & 8 HOURS

6 Month old:

THE AVERAGE BABY
NAPPED 3 HOURS A DAY

50%
OF BABIES
GOT BETWEEN
2.5 & 4.5 HOURS

96%
OF BABIES
GOT BETWEEN
0.5 & 4 HOURS

Month old:

HE AVERAGE BABY
APPED 2 HOURS A DAY

50%
OF BABIES
GOT BETWEEN
2 & 4 HOURS

96%
OF BABIES
GOT BETWEEN
0.5 & 4 HOURS

1 Year old:

THE AVERAGE BABY
SLEPT 2 HOURS A DAY

50%
OF BABIES
GOT BETWEEN
2 & 3 HOURS

96%
OF BABIES
GOT BETWEEN
0.5 & 3 HOURS

18 Months old:

THE AVERAGE BABY
NAPPED 1-2 HOURS A DAY

50%
OF BABIES
NAPPED FOR
2 HOURS

96%
OF BABIES
GOT BETWEEN
0.5 & 3 HOURS

Years old:

HE AVERAGE BABY
NAPPED 1 HOUR A DAY

50%
OF BABIES
GOT BETWEEN
1 & 3 HOURS

96%
OF BABIES
GOT BETWEEN
0.5 & 2 HOURS

IN A RECENT STUDY OF AMERICAN CHILDREN,
82% OF BABIES OVER 18 MONTHS WERE NOT
TAKING ANY NAPS ON SOME OR ALL DAYS.

CHAPTER 4 //
Infant Soap Opera

Infant Soap Opera //
A Messy Subject

D iapers and Potty Training. It's a dirty subject, but we have to cover it, so let's get going.

Right Diaper:

Use the right diaper for your baby, not for you. Saving a little cash is always fun, but diapers may not be the place to skim-out on for your savings account. #teamcleanandcomfortable

6-Pack:

Shop around as you're looking for the best diaper for your kid. Their size, movement and bathroom habits are all things to consider when shopping around. Buy small 6-packs at first and then begin the bulk shopping once you've found the right brand. Things to look for in the perfect diaper: a snug fit around the waist and legs, but not so tight that there are marks left behind. If your little one has allergies, look for a brand that comes sans plastic linings and perfumes.

Arm the Shields:

Prepare the shield because changing a baby is an investable water show. Regardless of gender, race, political affiliation, or the last time your baby ate, when you begin the diaper changing process, you will quickly learn that they love to pee as soon as the diaper comes off. They all do it. Maybe it's a human nature thing. A simple hack is to be prepared. Before you take off the diaper, have a towel ready so that when they squirt, you can protect yourself and the room.

Water Over Wipes:

When dealing with a rash, consider water over wipes. Luke-warm water on a soft tissue will reduce irritation, which can sometimes be a side effect of chemicals. Baby-approved ointment is also great for combatting rashes, but most babies hate how it feels. Instead of applying it, place the ointment on the diaper.

Battleship:

Homemade ship. When showering a six month old and older, you may be hesitant to sit them in the tub as they can be slippery. Instead, you can place a plastic basket into the tub, which serves as a better transition from the sink to baby baths in the grown up tub world.

Infant Soap Opera //
Potty Training

Done with diapers, so let's move on to potty training.

The Rewards Debate:

There are two schools of thought here: provide your little one with a reward for a successful potty experience or treat going to the bathroom like just any other part of life, which means not making a big deal out of it. Because every child is unique, it's impossible to know which ones will react well to positive reinforcement and which ones will see it as a silly gimmick. If you are going to use positive reinforcement, it is best to start out with a slightly extravagant reward like a new toy or ice cream and then gradually reduce the value of the reward until it becomes a kiss on the cheek.

Game Room:

Make the bathroom an inviting place. Let your toddler participate in the decoration process, allow them to put up a poster of their favorite characters and even keep some toys in there. That way when they have a sudden urge, there is no delay. The best way to make the bathroom inviting is to study your kid and see what he prefers in other rooms. Particular toys, sights and sounds are great places to begin.

Game Time:

For little boys, throwing in some stale cheerios into the toilet bowl makes for a fun way to have target practice. And while we're on the subject of cleanliness, a big discomfort for most parents is the washing of the hands. Because most toddlers tend to be short, you'll find yourself constantly carrying them at an awkward angle so they can wash their hands. This can easily be hacked by allowing them to wash their hands at the toddler level shower faucet. As always though, make sure you are paying close attention as it is never a smart move to leave a child and running water alone for a second. Once they outgrown the shower faucet, a sturdy stepping-stool can act as a great transitional support.

Crime and Punishment:

If 'accidents' are becoming a serious concern, turn the clean-up into a group project. If the issues persist, begin to have your child clean up the mess by themselves. Now, they won't do a good job, and you'll have to step in once they're "done" to finish the job. But human nature will begin to kick in and they'll grow a repulsion to the smell.

Bed Wetter:

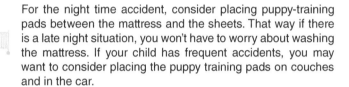

For the night time accident, consider placing puppy-training pads between the mattress and the sheets. That way if there is a late night situation, you won't have to worry about washing the mattress. If your child has frequent accidents, you may want to consider placing the puppy training pads on couches and in the car.

It's not going to be easy, it's not going to be fun, but it will be a lifelong memory that you'll carry with you and pull out at dinner parties for the next fifty years. As you begin the potty training process, you'll get frustrated from time to time. But always keep in mind that one day they're going to go off to college, and that day you'll do anything to go back to these potty training days…so try and make the best of them.

**Infant Soap Opera //
Shower Time**

The first bath can be a scary experience. The fact is your little one might not enjoy it either. But with a few hacks and some practice, bath time will quickly become one of your favorite parts of the week.

How Clean is Too Clean:

It's going to be hard to get those who suffer from Mysophobia to agree, but a daily bath isn't the best idea for a newborn. Mainly because bathing them more than three or four times a week can lead to a dried out baby. Instead, keep a close eye on their diapers and bibs. Cleaning them immediately will reduce the amount of baths you'll have to partake in early on.

Sponge Baby Square Pants:

Moms across the web swear by sponge baths over bathtubs during the first few weeks of your baby's life. For a quick an easy sponge bath, you'll need a few things.

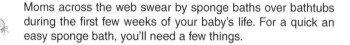

A flat surface in a relatively warm room. A work desk or kitchen counter covered with a towel or two make for a suitable area.

A shallow bin or bucket with warm water. Roughly 100 F.

Have the washcloth, cotton balls and a diaper with the change of clothes handy in order to reduce the amount of time your baby will be exposed.

Once your baby is ready, wrap them up in a towel to keep them warm. Then using the moist washcloth, softly brush their face. Keep in mind that during these first few baths you will not need to use soap. Instead grab a damp cotton ball and use it to clean their eyes, ears and cheeks. As you move into the body, make sure to keep your baby covered except for the part you are cleaning. Focus in particular on the areas where there are creases that could hide dirt.

Final Word on Staying Clean:

Safety is the number one priority on all things related to your baby. Under no circumstances should you ever leave your child unattended during a cleaning.

CHAPTER 5 //
Fevers and Safety

**Fevers and Safety //
Paging Dr. Parent**

There are few things as scary as your child's first fever. Before we get into the hacks for handling a sick child, always remember that fevers and colds are fairly common when it comes to kids; especially, once they start interacting with other children. So without further ado, let's hack colds, fevers, coughs and aches.

Hack Cheat-Sheet:

 Infections, which tend to lead to fevers, are as common as finding Candy Crush on a stranger's iPhone.

 Fevers tend to last 72 hours, but that can disappear in 24 or make it to about 96 hours. Once you start creeping into the triple digits, it might be time to get to a hospital.

 You don't generally need to track your fever-stricken baby's temperature every half hour. But make sure to speak with their pediatrician in order to establish how many times the good doctor would like you to check it. #digitalthermometer

 A cold compress on their forehead is always a good place to start fighting back.

 Cover the baby in layers so it is easy to manage their internal temperature.

 Fluids, fluids and more fluids.

Call the Doctor:

There are a handful of signs that should trigger you contacting the pediatrician.

 A temperature of 104 F or higher

A baby less than 12 weeks old with a temperature over 100.4

 A fever over 24 hours when a baby is under 24 months

 Physical pain symptoms like ear pain, a sore throat and/or stiff body.

Fevers and Safety //
At the Doctor's Office

Thanks to the advancements of modern medicine, children re-
ceive more vaccines than ever before. With all these added
shots, it's no wonder why one of the biggest fears among children is
doctor visits. So how can you hack this fear?

Reasoning:

It's widely accepted that the inherent intelligence of a child
is generally overlooked. Avoid making that mistake by taking opportunities to reason with your child. A great chance
for this give and take development exists prior to a medical
exam. Most children will be fearful of the unknown when it
comes to doctors. Explaining to them in simple and informa-
tive terms can ease their tension.

Quick and Painless:

While it will seem difficult at first, try and fill doctor visit days
with as many activities as possible. It can definitely stretch
your parental time management skills, but it comes with a
huge payoff. By jam-packing the activities your child will partake in, you'll eliminate the fear. Your child will be too preoc-
cupied with what they are doing, what they've already done
and what they will do after the doctor to fully analyze their
fear. So schedule a doctor visit the same day your little one
has daycare, a visit to their favorite store and a sleepover at
night.

Simple Solution:

We're with you. Keeping their schedule full can be hard to
keep up with on every visit. For those times when you can't
hack it, look for help. Books, toys and the modern marvel that
is the tablet are all good ways to keep their fears at bay while
you sit in the waiting room.

**Fevers and Safety //
Home Remedies**

Doctor visits aren't always needed. For the smaller aches and pains, there are few things better than Nana's remedy passed down from generation to generation. So here are the remedies we found to be the most recommended and time-tested.

Really Stuffed Up = Steamy, Herb-Filled Air:

Breathing soft, moist air helps relax the mucus in the nasal passages. You'll need a humidifier, cool-mist vaporizer, or steamy bathroom. For a very stuffy nose, add in some mint leaves, which help in clearing out the passages.

General Congestion = Vapor Rub:

For congested children who are more than twelve weeks old and are having a hard time getting rest, vapor rub is a great place to start. Now this is tricky because science says that there is no direct correlation between the rub's natural ingredients and nasal congestion…but they worked, so if you're a believer in placebos, this is a remedy that can't be missed.

Cough = Bees Knees:

This hack too comes with a prerequisite of at least twelve months. For any child over the age of one who has a terrible throat and cough, honey might be the best solution. Honey coats and relaxes the throat, which gets irritated as you cough. If the flavor is something your little one just cannot handle, consider placing a couple drops of lemon over the top.

Warts = Good ol' Duct Tape:

Warts can be a nuisance that many parents struggle to combat. A fun and easy way to remove them painlessly is to use duct tape. Simply place a small square of it against the wart and leave it there for a couple of weeks. Make sure to change it if it gets really dirty. But the idea is to leave it on as long as possible. Without being able to breathe and without room to grow, the wart will simply fall off.

Nosebleeds = Cayenne:

Now that we are thinking out side of the box let's look at nose-bleeds. All the parents we spoke to swore by this remedy. This thick and spicy powder can help a nosebleed stop because, well we don't know why, but there's plenty of evidence of it working. The idea is that you place the powder on a cotton ball and then dab it around the nostril. Magically the bleeding stops. Let's hope the sneezing doesn't begin.

Anxiety = Bubble Fun:

Children's anxiety is something that medicine has only recently begun to examine. Unfortunately, that means that there aren't a lot of ways to combat it. However, small studies have found that playing with bubbles helps relax a child. So if your toddler is acting out and you're not sure why, they may be going through some anxiety, which would be a good time to get them relaxing with some bubbles.

Ear Infections = Blow Dryer:

As a child who grew up in a pool, my mother kept a gallon jug of the pink stuff around. Some ear infections were worse than oth-ers, but they were always uncomfortable, annoying and painful. If your child gets these, a good way to avoid an infection is to get the water out immediately. Use a blow dryer at the medium setting within a foot or so between their ear and the air, and simply evaporate the water out.

Car Sickness = Ginger:

This hack is particularly cool because it works on children, adults, and animals. A little bit of ginger (either raw in small slices or in water) will eliminate any sort of motion sickness. So next time you have a long drive ahead, a ride on a rollercoaster or a tummy-troubled pup, make sure to go to the ginger.

**Fevers and Safety //
Baby Proofing**

Yay! Your baby's crawling, moving, and one step closer to college. They grow up so fast. With each small step comes one more thing to focus on. Now that your little one is mobile, it's time to secure your house. There are two options when it comes to baby-proofing a house. **1)** bubble-wrap your baby, or **2)** follow our hacks. Traditionally, proofing a house can be time-consuming, expensive and fairly useless. So we've taken all the junk out and put together the simplest, most efficient and beneficial hacks to keeping your little bundle of joy as safe as possible.

Pool Noodles:

A summertime staple, pool noodles are cost-conscious and effective. A few pool noodles, cut up, taped and sealed can turn any coffee table corner into a padded edge without any repercussions on the furniture.

If your local stores aren't carrying any pool noodles because it's not summer, you can still cover up the sharp corners with budget-friendly tennis balls.

Water Time Play Dough:

Door knobs, handles, and protruding hoses all tend to be made of very hard steel materials. Molding them in play-doh allows for accidental bumps to not scrape. In particular while in a shower, wrapping the hot and cold knobs with the dough seems like a good idea.

If you don't have play-doh at hand, grabbing an old pair of tube socks tends to be a solid backup. Although they don't handle the water as well.

Prison Break:

A major safety concern for parents is when their baby begins to explore the crib culminating in their great escape. Major head bumps can be avoided with a small piece of fabric. Simply sew a small connection on the onesie legs so that your baby can still move, but if they attempt to raise one leg over the banister, they won't be able to.

Bite Proof:

A teething baby will gnaw on just about anything. From tables (which we noodle-proofed) to their crib, your little one will bite down on anything to relieve their gum pain. Now if you spent a shiny penny on the crib, the last thing you want is for it to look like it came with a hungry mouse. You can easily use a clean blanket to wrap around the bannister. That will prevent your baby's teeth from ruining the crib.

A Familiar Trick, Redone:

A time-tested home safety hack is to use hair ties or rubber bands to keep cabinets closed. However, conventional wisdom will teach you that bands tend to snap. By removing one injury you may inadvertently cause another one. But if you own twisty-ties (and honestly who doesn't?), replace the risky bands and hair ties with twisty ties. If your ties are not long enough, use a shoelace as an extender.

Electric Shield:

A surge protector is great for a storm and for providing added outlets. But to a baby, it's just another thing to taste. To avoid any sort of catastrophe, grab an old piece of Tupperware and arrange it so that it acts as a cage around the surge protector. Not only will this keep your baby safe, but it'll keep dust out of it, as well.

While we're on this power surge, use duct tape to cover power outlets. It's not fancy, it's not clever, it's just efficient. Do it.

It's a beautifully sunny day outside, yet you might be worried about taking your baby into the world. There is a common misconception that a newborn should stay inside for the first few weeks. However, there's no science to back that up. The truth is a baby can go out into the world a few days after birth, so long as it's showing all the normal signs of being healthy. If your child was born prematurely or if their immune system may be under-developed, it is best to consult the doctor on a timeline. From sun-shining naps to joyous laughter under a sunset, fresh air, clouds, and natural light are excellent for anyone, including babies. Interestingly enough, in Europe, a community of hospitals place newborns outside for short bursts on a daily basis. **So grab your little one, pack a bag and enjoy the great outdoors!**

CHAPTER 6 //
Baby Meets World

**Baby Meets World //
Strollers**

Strollers today are more than just four wheels and a seat. From filtered canopies to seat warmers and yes, even Wi-Fi, buying a stroller is far more complicated than ever before. A basic one that adjusts to your baby's ever changing size, with reliable wheels and comfortable chair won't be too hard to find. But if you're the hipster parent that wants to truly stand out as you order your pressed coffee at the local shop, you'll want to consider these accessories.

Strapped In:

There are a collection of varying brands, but they all tend to have similar high reviews and the same product promise. It's essentially a Velcro strap made to secure anything and everything your child might play with as they sit in the stroller. From bottles to pacifiers to their favorite toy, these straps adjust to the item so that if they get tossed, they'll never hit the floor and get lost.

Hooked:

Whether you're taking your little one to the local farmer's market or your neighborhood pharmacy, carrying bags can become difficult. This minor setback can easily be corrected with aluminum hooks that attach to nearly any stroller and allow for bags to be hung.

Keep in mind that if you're operating a light-weight stroller, the bags could eventually outweigh the stroller and cause it to topple over. If this is a concern, simple gym-training ankle weights can be added to the stroller for added weight.

Organizer 2.0:

From your phone to your water bottle to your house keys, carrying essentials while taking your baby out can be difficult. For fathers without purses, consider using a stroller organizer. They come in different shapes, sizes and colors but they all tend to do the same thing: hold and organize your essentials.

SPF:

Most parents' biggest concern when taking their baby out is the sun. There are sunscreens out there that claim to be for infants, but the FDA recommends keeping sunscreen off babies entirely. So what are you to do? Canopy! There a re wildly expensive canopy additions that are universal for strollers, but a well-kept umbrella tends to do the trick. Any sort of makeshift shade you can provide will not only protect their sensitive skin from the sun, but it will keep them a few degrees cooler, as well.

From practicality to just the absurd, these add-ons are a quirky way to solve minor hiccups that come along with sharing your baby with the world.

Baby Meets World //
Baby Seats

The two biggest concerns for new parents: cars and pools. Sadly, these two are responsible for more infant deaths than any other form of accidents. With cars in particular there is no room for hacks and shortcuts. The following are just the top recommendations as provided by the Mayo Clinic and the Safe Kids Organization.

Before we begin, make sure you understand your car and the seat you buy. The biggest decision is knowing if you are buying a front-facing chair or a rear-facing chair. Also keep in mind that, on average, a child will outgrow a rear-facing seat at 24 months, although it will vary among children.

Labeling:

Pay attention to the label on the car seat to assure that it is appropriate for your child's age, weight and height. Most people don't know this, but baby seats come with expiration dates, so keep an eye out for the date.

History and Buying Used:

The most important thing to consider when buying a used car seat is its accident history. Basically, only buy a used one from someone you know and not just the thrift store around the corner or the internet. The logic is that a car seat is only designed to protect from one accident.

Installations:

After you have installed the chair, yank it with some force. If the chair is properly installed, it will not give more than an inch. If your chair buckles more than that, remove it and reinstall. Besides the inch test, you can use a pinch to assure that your child fits correctly within the chair. Make sure the harness is buckled tightly. Once the chest clips are set by the armpit, pinch the strap over your child's shoulder. You should not be able to grasp any excess webbing in a properly fitted chair.

Booster Chair:

How do you know if your little one is ready to make the climb from a baby chair to a booster? Start by checking the car seats height and weight limits. If they are illegible, check your kid's shoulders to see if they are above the car seat's top harness slots. Still unsure? Are their ears above the top of the car seat?

Hot Cars:

Just don't do it. There is never a reason, and nothing in the world tempting enough to consider leaving a napping baby alone in a hot car for a second. A car's temperature can shoot up 15 degrees in an instant, and a million other unimaginable things can occur in between. There is just no need to even consider it.

Bulk:

On the other hand, in a winter wonderland you'll find yourself bundling your baby with as many layers as possible. However, the layers can affect how effective the safety features of the chair will be. Instead, dress your baby normally and then place blankets over the chair.

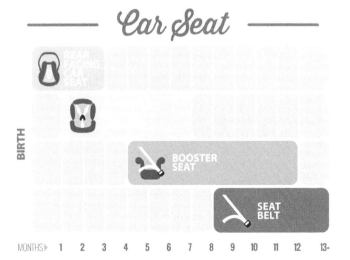

Baby Meets World //
Beach Body

Now that your little one is out on the open road let's head to beaches, landscapes and monuments. After all, this world is filled with amazing locals to share with your bundle of joy. An easy first family trip is to the beach. Sand, water, and the fresh ocean breeze all hit your little one in an instant causing a wonderful sensory overload which is usually met with laughter. Sunscreen was covered earlier, but a quick recap is to not apply sunblock to any baby under 6 months. Instead, keep them in the shade. Whether you are considering taking them into the water or not, make sure they are dressed in easily breathable clothes.

For a toddler that will be getting sunscreen, keep these notes in mind.

Any section not protected by clothes and/or a hat should have a thick layer of sunscreen placed.

Ideally place the sunscreen on before you head to the beach and then again upon arriving.

The SPF should be a minimum of 15 and should be marked to be for children under a certain age.

The broad-spectrum brand should have a four-star or five-star rating. This guarantees that it offers UVA and UVB protection.

Reapply, reapply, and reapply after they go in the water, if they are sweating and every few hours.

Besides sunscreen, what else will your baby need?

Towels, of course. Windbreakers can also help when attending the beach on a particularly windy day where sand can get kicked up. If you have an adventurous crawler or walking toddler, they also help keep your little one from wandering too far away. While we have sand on our mind, it can irritate a baby if it sits between their chunky rolls. So bringing a towel to have a layer separating the sand from the skin is always a good idea.

Safety and comfort at the beach can be planned for and will quickly make your beach trip that much more enjoyable.

Rising Tide:

Set up camp away from the water because as the tide comes, you won't want to be packing your towels and blankets and food. And there is the double benefit of not having run after wayward toddlers too quickly.

Seasoned with Sand:

Kids in general love tasting stuff. That won't change at the beach. If your little one gets a hold of sand, get ready because they're about to taste it. Pacifiers are a good way to keep their mouths occupied. But if they do end up tasting the sand, make sure you keep them from swallowing it. A little water here can help.

Hazard Flags:

You can take your little one into the ocean, so long as there are no major warnings. Things like jellyfish sightings, strong currents or other hazards should be taken very seriously. If you find yourself at the beach without being able to share the water with your baby, you can always build them a small puddle-pool. Simply dig out a small hole, use a bucket or cup to bring water from the ocean and safely place your tiny tot in the water.

**Baby Meets World //
Jet Set**

W orking backwards on our ABCs, we've covered cars and beaches, so now let's head abroad. The main thing to consider when traveling is your child's age. Any baby under six months won't have the proper immunizations to visit certain parts of the world. Any land where exotic diseases may be prevalent will have to be rescheduled for a later time. Also, for some reason, ski resorts (and romantic island-paradise type resorts) tend to not offer accommodations for babies of a certain age. It is best to check with them prior to booking. One last thing to run by your doctor before taking your baby on a flight is the altitude of where you'll be traveling to. Altitude can affect a multiple of things within your body, so it is best to run these questions by them before boarding.

Let's get going!

Long flights can be combatted with a few helpful tools. Of course, toys can be a happy distraction, but when they don't work, try your hand at these:

Crayons:

Scribbling, drawing, coloring, anything really that keeps them focused on a pen and paper will make the flight seem that much faster.

Gadgets:

Not necessarily movies or television shoes, but instead music or repetitive images. These items will keep your baby focused better than a program with lot of fancy images and dialog.

Education:

It's never too early to get some learning on. You can read to your child, share in an ad-libs game and even consider some trivia.

Ear Popping:

A hack most parents seem to love is the pacifier or feeding hack for when you ascend and descend. This sucking action will reduce the uncomfortable ear sensation that can make any baby irritable.

Once you've arrived at your destination consider purchasing a low-priced stroller. There is no need to haul a bulky stroller around, especially since some airlines will consider it a checked bag and incur the fees that come with actual luggage. And you definitely do not want to be carrying your baby everywhere you go. After all, you are on vacation.

Baby Meets World //
Digital Baby

W e're just about done, but this wouldn't be a hack book without looking at all the digital advancements that are in place to make raising your baby an easy and fun adventure.

Pre and post-pregnancy, you'll always want to have the WebMD app. It pretty much covers any question you may have in regards to your baby and the next 20+ years of their life.

 Baby Piano for a newborn is a great musical and sound recognition game that is interactive and educational.

 Restroom Finder does exactly that. And whether you're constantly needing to find a bathroom as a pregnant parent or you're looking for somewhere to change your newborn, this app will always come in handy.

 iBaby Phone allows you to let your baby play with your phone without them being able to accidentally dial, delete or retweet anything.

 Milestone apps are all over smart phone digital stores. They allow you to track major accomplishments such as first tooth, first steps and of course, first word. But beyond that you can check your progress with medically-backed stats on averages with certain milestones. Plus, some include features to track milk and diet consumptions.

 During the first week, your doctor will want you to track anything and everything your baby does and how often they do it. There are great apps like Total Baby that serve this perfectly.

So now that you have all these apps. When can you share them? It is something that parents debate about constantly, but what's the right answer for letting your child play and eventually become addicted to the digital world?

The AAP first issued technology advice for infants back in 1999. Since the 90s, more research has been done and the findings remain the same. Any child under 2 years of age will not benefit in any way from TV or video games. There might be some stimulation of the senses, but not enough to combat the reality that the stimulation might do more harm than good. So while apps and shows exists with the disclaimer of "safe for children under two," the reality is that there are better ways to entertain and bond with your baby.

A NOTE FROM THE AUTHORS

Parenting is not a game. It's definitely not a joke. So please take these hacks with a grain of salt, unless you have high blood pressure. The truth is that these hacks are well researched and semi-tested, but we are definitely not parenting experts. Most of these hacks developed from conversations with our parents, our in-laws and the occasional mother of four juggling groceries, a briefcase and twin infants on her way to her mini-van outside of Whole Foods. We hope you give them a shot, tweet the ones you love and write to us about the ones that seemed silly to you and through it all, remember to have fun. Enjoy your new bundle of joy and congratulations!

DATA SOURCES

http://hushp.harvard.edu/sites/default/files/downloadable_files/IFHPComparativePriceReport.pdf

http://www.alternet.org/economy/babies-are-expensive

http://www.bbc.com/news/business-31052665

http://americanpregnancy.org/pregnancy-health/exercise-guidelines/

http://www.acog.org/Resources-And-Publications/Committee-Opinions/Committee-on-Obstetric-Practice/Exercise-During-Pregnancy-and-the-Postpartum-Period

https://infogr.am/three-trimesters-of-pregnancy-by-trisha-singh

http://www.mayoclinic.org/healthy-living/infant-and-toddler-health/expert-answers/newborn/faq-20057752

http://www.cdc.gov/Motorvehiclesafety/child_passenger_safety/cps-factsheet.html

http://www.parentingscience.com/baby-sleep-requirements.html

http://www.safercar.gov/parents/CarSeats/Right-Seat-Age-And-Size-Recommendations.htm

OTHER SOURCES

http://www.nerdwallet.com/blog/health/2014/04/16/pregnant-maternity-coverage-benefits/

http://www.nytimes.com/2013/07/01/health/ameri   can-way-of-birth-costliest-in-the-world.html?pagewanted=all&_r=0

http://www.webmd.com/baby/guide/first-trimester-of-pregnancy?page=2

http://www.webmd.com/baby/guide/health-baby-second-trimester

http://www.fitpregnancy.com/exercise/prenatal-workouts/5-simple-pregnancy-exercises-every-trimester/slide/6

http://www.webmd.com/baby/guide/third-trimester-of-pregnancy

http://www.babycentre.co.uk/a536346/herbal-remedies-in-pregnancy

http://med.stanford.edu/news/all-news/2010/02/acupuncture-lessens-depression-symptoms-during-pregnancy-study-shows.html

http://www.adoptuskids.org/for-families/how-to-adopt

http://www.parents.com/baby/development/intellectual/simple-ways-to-make-baby-smarter/

http://familydoctor.org/familydoctor/en/pregnancy-newborns/caring-for-newborns/breastfeeding-formula/breastfeeding-hints-to-help-you-get-off-to-a-good-start.html

http://www.parents.com/baby/breastfeeding/tips/tips-getting-baby-breastfeeding/

http://healthfinder.gov/HealthTopics/Category/parenting/nutrition-and-physical-activity/eat-healthy-while-breastfeeding-quick-tips

http://www.quickanddirtytips.com/parenting/babies-infants/diaper-tips?page=1

http://www.webmd.com/cold-and-flu/treat-symptoms-12/treat-fever-young-children

http://www.fda.gov/ForConsumers/ConsumerUpdates/ucm309136.htm

http://www.mayoclinic.org/healthy-living/infant-and-toddler-health/in-depth/car-seat-safety/art-20043939?pg=1

http://www.safekids.org/tip/car-seat-tips

CPSIA information can be obtained at www.ICGtesting.com
Printed in the USA
BVOW11s0130160415

396373BV00004B/13/P